This book is dedicated
to my loving wife Holly
and beautiful daughter Cassidy.

Once you've seen the magnificence, and heard the music produced by a waterfall, it is something you will never forget.

A Tetra Press Book

Published in the USA by Tetra SecondNature,
3001 Commerce Street, Blacksburg, VA 24060

© 1997 Tranquility Ponds

ISBN 1-56465-195-9
Item No: WL 16010

All correspondence concerning the content of this volume
should be addressed to Tetra SecondNature.
Contact Tetra Press at Tetra SecondNature
1-800-526-0650
http://www.tetra-fish.com/aboutus.html

Printed in China

The Complete Guide
HOW TO BUILD
PONDS & WATERFALLS

By Jeffrey Reid

THANK YOU: First I want to thank the loving, forgiving, and understanding Lord Jesus Christ, my wife Holly and my daughter Cassidy for being patient and supportive, and all of the wonderful people who made this book possible; John Gluntz, Pat Kellas, Dustin Wilson, Greg Hall, David Plant, Carolyn Gluntz, Greg Hodge, Jason Beer, Denis & Jody Benson and the Shafer family.

COPY EDITOR: Mary Klein

DESIGN & PRODUCTION: Workhorse Production, Inc.

WL 16010

Contents

The Complete Guide
How To Build Ponds & Waterfalls

19 - Pond Placement

42 - Waterfall Building

54 - Pond Plants

Introduction

Adding a pond or waterfall to your landscape will be one of the most rewarding things you'll ever do. I fell in love with their significant beauty about twelve years ago and I've never looked back. Water features, many of which are in this book, have brought me so much personal joy and pleasure. Knowing the correct steps and using the right product for the job practically guarantees success. This book will show and tell you everything that you need. The methods shown in these chapters are proven and have been taught to thousands of do-it-yourselfers.

Jeffrey Reid

Site Selection

The #1 guideline to use when selecting a site for your water feature is simple. Put the pond where it will give you the most enjoyment.

However, this need not apply to every situation. Entryway ponds or perhaps a water feature in the middle of a circular driveway are also wonderful options.

Also important is the overall view of the pond. Where is the main vantage point from which the water feature will be viewed? It could be your deck or patio, living room window or perhaps a sunroom. If you are planning a stream or waterfall, now is the time to decide on its placement. The pond's vantage point has every-

Notice how this waterfall is at the back of the pond (best for viewing). This is a beautiful example of a backyard pond with all the elements: moving water, aquatic plants and, if you look closely, you can see the colorful fish under the lily pads.

thing to do with the placement of the waterfall.

Moving water demands attention and breathes life into any landscape. The focal point is the waterfall. This is the highlight of the pond and should always be placed at the back of the pond.

Sunlight

Be aware of how much sunlight the area receives. As a general rule, the amount of sunlight should not dictate the pond's location. Sunlight can be as positive as it is negative, which is why it is not much of a consideration.

What is the ideal amount of sunlight? There is no specific correct answer. More sunlight means more blooms on your flowering plants (water lilies, water iris, etc.). It may also mean more of a problem with algae. Less sunlight means less bloom, but foliage is generally greener and more lush (not burned by the sun). There are many water plant varieties that are quite shade tolerant; such as, bog bean, water hawthorn, and marsh marigold.

Providing shade for the pond is important and can be done in a variety of ways. Planting large trees on the south side of the pond can provide a great deal of shade in

Deciding on a place to put your water feature is probably the biggest decision you'll make, along with its size. It's not uncommon for someone to rebuild their water feature within the first year because they later decide it would be even more enjoyable if it were larger. Make these decisions early on in the planning stages.

the morning or afternoon depending on their exact placement. Plants that cover the surface of the pond (water lilies, hyacinths, and water lettuce) help to shade the water.

Another way that has become very popular in recent years is dyeing the water. By using a nontoxic UV sunscreen, you can change the color of the water. Dye colors available are blue, black and brown and, of course, the darker you go the more effective the dye is at keeping the UV rays out of the water. Most pond dyes dissipate every four to six weeks so it will be necessary to add more every now and then. Fortunately these dyes are inexpensive.

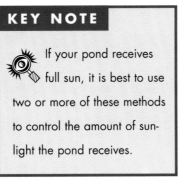

KEY NOTE

If your pond receives full sun, it is best to use two or more of these methods to control the amount of sunlight the pond receives.

The large trees that surround this pond provide shade as well as a wonderful background.

When a fish pond is out in the middle of the yard, some steps should be taken to protect it from the sun.

Trees

For the most part trees are not a deterrent during pond placement consideration. There are, however, extreme circumstances where there are just too many large trees in a small area. The positive side to having large trees next to the pond is that they can provide some valuable shade and they look great. The down side is that deciduous trees will drop leaves in the fall. Of course, this nuisance only lasts one or two months of the year. You can purchase a pond skimmer for approximately fifteen dollars to eliminate problems caused by falling leaves or needles. Some

KEY NOTE

Fallen leaves left in the pond over winter can be dangerous to the ecology of your pond. As the warmer temperature of spring approaches, the leaves begin to decompose and will pollute the pond.

people choose to net the entire pond, which works well at keeping the leaves out. Unfortunately, it is usually unsightly. If you choose this method, you should only leave the net up through fall. Top water skimmers are also available, however, they are difficult to install.

It is not necessary to have a lot of height for a waterfall. This peaceful stream is twenty feet long, yet drops only 2 feet.

Slope

Will the pond be built on a slope? While a slope is most desirable for a stream or waterfall, not so with a pond. Since the biggest key to developing a beautiful pond is controlling the finished water level, a slope can make this more of a challenge. If you are going to build on a slope, here is a helpful demonstration.

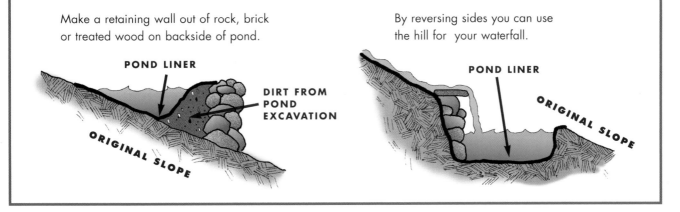

BUILDING ON A SLOPE

Make a retaining wall out of rock, brick or treated wood on backside of pond.

POND LINER

DIRT FROM POND EXCAVATION

ORIGINAL SLOPE

By reversing sides you can use the hill for your waterfall.

POND LINER

ORIGINAL SLOPE

Types of ponds

FORMAL: Formal water features are almost always the main focal point of the landscape. There are different styles of formal ponds. These ponds are based on exact shapes such as circles or squares. Formal ponds oftentimes include ornaments or statuary. A fountain in the middle of a formal pond is a common sight and will help draw attention to the pond with its visual beauty and sound.

NATURAL: Natural or informal ponds are meant to blend in with the natural (native) landscape of the area rather than stand out. Regardless, even the most natural pond is still going to be the focal point of the landscape.

Designing a natural pond is fun and stress free since irregular shapes are not the exception, they are the rule. From winding curves to oblong lines your personal expression is the guideline.

This foamy fountain contributes to the sound as well as the look of this formal pond.

The type of rock, water plants and landscaping used all contribute to this natural beauty.

Formal Shapes

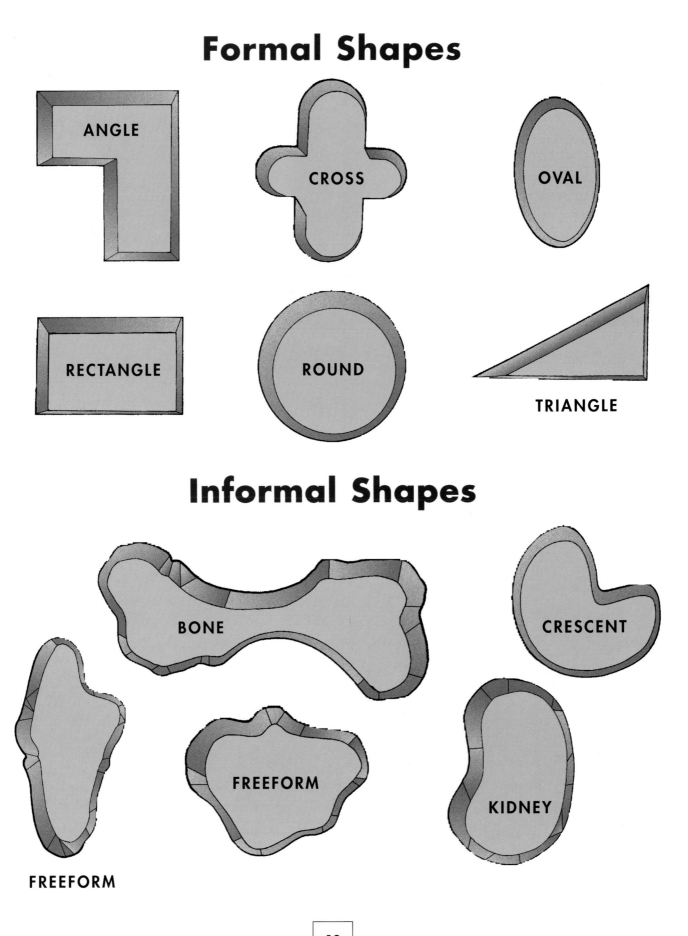

ANGLE

CROSS

OVAL

RECTANGLE

ROUND

TRIANGLE

Informal Shapes

BONE

CRESCENT

FREEFORM

KIDNEY

FREEFORM

18

Landscape design examples that involve pond and waterfall placement.

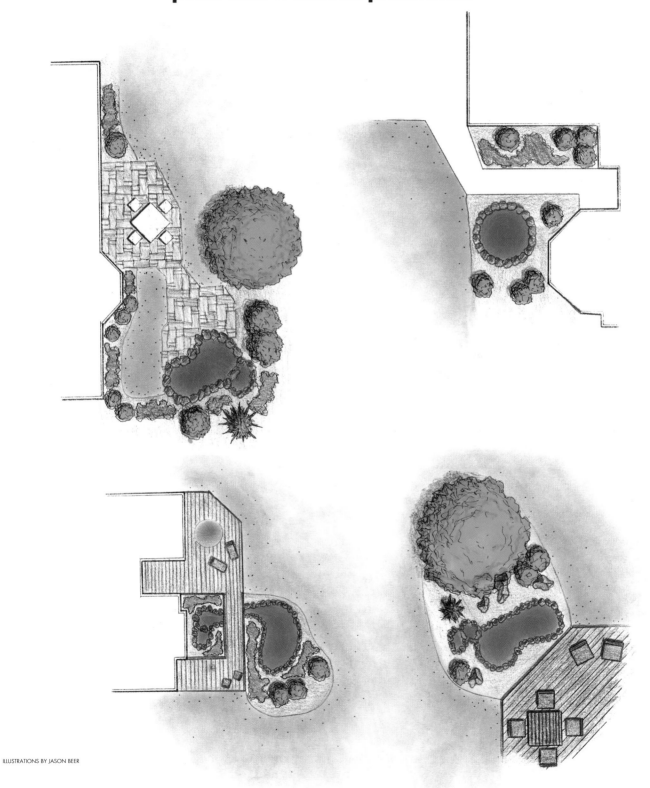

ILLUSTRATIONS BY JASON BEER

Materials and Products

When it comes to building your pond, there is much available from which to choose. Building your pond is something you want to do only once. If you know the proper steps (Pages 28–48), and you use the correct material, your pond will be a great success. Since everyone's situation will vary, here are some of your options.

By using a flexible liner you can build any free form shape you like.

Pond Lining Materials

FLEXIBLE POND LINER: Far and away the material of choice for the do-it-yourselfer. You are not limited to a specific size or shape as you are with the preformed shells. Also there is no mess and much less margin for error than when pouring a concrete pond.

Pliable liners such as polyurethane, polyvinylchloride (PVC), butyl or EPDM rubber give you ultimate flexibility in your design making your imagination your only limit.

There are some very important keys to remember, if you are going to build a liner pond. Although there are many pond liners available, search out a quality liner with a long life expectancy and a good reputation for being durable. The pond liner you choose should not be based only on its price, but on its quality.

Never seam two liners together to form one big pond liner. It is all right to use two separate liners, when one is being used for the pond and the other for the waterfall. Pond liners come with special glues and tapes that make mending liners together possible, however, if there is going to be a leakage problem it will start at the taped seam. It is always best to use one solid piece of liner for the pond to eliminate any possibility of this problem occurring.

Making special shapes and designs that are uniquely yours is a lot of fun.

MEASURING FOR YOUR LINER

Measuring your pond to be fitted for a flexible liner: Add depth twice to length and width then add at least one foot to both numbers to allow for liner overhang.

POND SIZE

Longest x Widest x Deepest

10' x 8' x 2'

LINER SIZE

15' x 13'

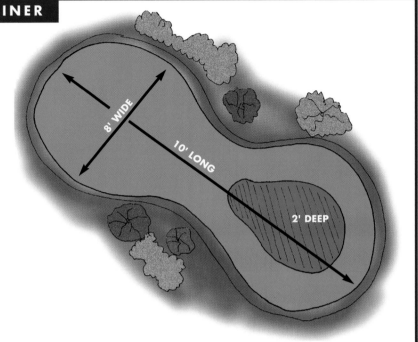

Certain brands of flexible liners are available in single sheets up to an acre in size, making large ponds like this one possible.

Preformed pond shells are available in a wide variety of shapes. Here are a couple examples. Notice that the one on the right has a marginal shelf for planting.

This pond was built using a flexible liner. A more formal look was achieved by mortaring flat stones around the entire border.

Preformed ponds are molded of plastic or fiberglass and both are quality material. Installed properly, preformed ponds can be made to look very natural or entirely formal depending on the style and shape you choose. As with any pond, the #1 rule is leveling. Install a preformed pond perfectly level and it will look great.

Irish moss grows right over the edge of the pond. This is a perfect way to conceal the hard edge of a preform pond.

CONCRETE PONDS: In most respects, concrete is the least desirable material to use in pond construction. It is much more physically demanding, messy, and the most expensive choice.

In colder climates concrete should never be a consideration. Even with all the extra work and money that goes into their construction, they rarely hold water for more than a year or two before they crack due to freezing temperatures. However, if you choose to build a concrete pond, it is advisable to sandwich a pond liner in the concrete. Concrete ponds perform much better in warmer climates. If you decide on concrete, gunite, the highest

This waterfall is completely mortared in. In addition, there is also a flexible liner under the entire stream just in case the mortar cracks. By doing this, a leaky waterfall should never be an issue.

quality concrete, is very rich and needs to be applied by a professional.

BENTONITE (CLAY PONDS): Bentonite is an inexpensive way to go. That's the good news. Bentonite ponds are a long shot to be water tight. That's the bad news. On very large stocking ponds or golf courses this can be a cost effective alternative. If there is a constant water source (such as a year-round stream), then a clay bottom pond may be an alternative, since some

water loss won't be a big factor. Before choosing bentonite, have your soil checked to see if it will work with the clay.

Pumps

CENTRIFUGAL: These pumps sit outside the pond. They must be hidden and are somewhat difficult to plumb. Also, most don't come with power cords and need to be hard wired directly to the power source.

SUBMERSIBLE: Made for the do-it-yourselfer. It is very easy to hook them up to your waterfall or fountain plumbing. Submersible pumps are also easy to conceal. They sit inside the pond (under the water surface) usually at the bottom of the pond.

When choosing a pump there are a few things to consider. If you are using the pump to operate a biological filter, the pump you select should have the capacity to circulate the pond's water volume as recommended. The filter is not the only factor involved in selecting a pump. Different volumes of water will have quite a varying effect aesthetically and as far as sound is concerned. Using a larger volume pump on a waterfall can give you a white water show. The beautiful sound the flowing water provides can drown out local traffic or other undesirable noises. Be sure the pump you purchase is rated for twenty-four hour a day usage.

A large centrifugal pump is used here to produce a massive cascade of water. This type of extreme effect is best achieved by using a large centrifugal pump, since they are generally less expensive to run than sump pumps.

Plumbing

Just the word plumbing strikes fear into the hearts of most do-it-yourselfers, however, plumbing your pond need not be difficult at all. Choosing the plumbing material you use is an important decision.

Pipe Comparison

CORRUGATED FLEX PIPE: This product is superior in every way to all of its competition. It is designed specifically for ponds and is everything you could ask of a plumbing pipe and more. The pipe is corrugated on the outside and smooth bore on the inside. As you twist and shape it, it never kinks. Furthermore, it is UV protected and dark in color making it easy to conceal. It is very simple to install.

PVC PIPE: PVC pipe has one advantage over corrugated flex pipe. It's about half the price, but the advantages stop there. You are limited by 45

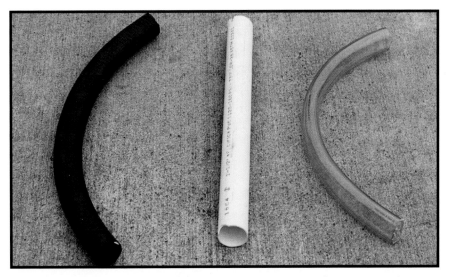

This picture shows the three different types of plumbing for your pond. From left to right: Corrugated flex pipe, PVC pipe, and Clear flex tube.

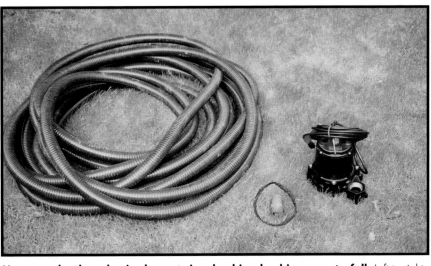

Here are the three basic elements involved in plumbing a waterfall. Left to right: Corrugated flex hose, male adapter (to connect the pipe to the pump), and the sump pump.

degree and 90 degree angles. The pipe is very rigid which makes installation more difficult. PVC can be very challenging to hide and is not UV protected.

CLEAR FLEX TUBE: Similar only in name to the flex pipe.

While the clear flex tube is easy to bend and shape it is not corrugated so, like a garden hose, it kinks. It is not UV protected. This means the sun's rays will break it down and destroy it causing leaks.

Even during the noon hour, the reflection on the surface of this still pond is as vivid as a painting.

PORTLAND JAPANESE GARDENS

Pond Building

By following the step-by-step program of this chapter, it will be easy for you to achieve this kind of success.

The truth is; the difference between a pond that "didn't turn out" and one that is "absolutely gorgeous" is four to five steps. If you know these steps, you will have great success.

This chapter will focus on liner and preformed ponds. Liners are far and away the most popular material to use today.

THE BENEFITS OF A LINER POND:

- Any shape, depth and size. There's virtually no limit to what you can do.
- Cost effective when compared to other materials.
- Easy and fun to work with.

CALCULATING POND CAPACITY

Rectangular Ponds

Length (') x Width x Depth = Volume in Cubic Feet

Cubic Feet x 7.5 = Total Gallons

Example: 10' long x 10' wide x 2' deep x 7.5 = 1,500 Gallons

1. The pond must be level. This is the difference between amateur and professional.

2. Always use one solid piece of pond liner. Although most manufacturers have glues and tapes that accompany their liners for making seams, it is not recommended.

3. Always use liner underneath the waterfall (liner under everything you do).

4. Protect the pond liner from any soil that might contain rocks, roots, or other debris. You can do this by using sand, an old carpet, or cardboard under the liner. There are also special

underlayment liners available made just for this purpose.

5. Never trim the liner until you have filled the pond with water. The same applies to the waterfall. Only then will you know exactly what level is and be able to trim accurately.

The above pond and waterfall show it is not necessary to have a large pond. A small pond can be equally as beautiful. In designing your water feature keep in mind it should fit the yard, or area of the yard, where you put it. In other words, putting a large pond in a small area may not leave enough room for landscaping. By putting a small pond in a large yard it may be lost in the surrounding landscape and not appreciated for what it is.

Step by step

Step #1 After deciding on the placement of the pond, next is the shape. By laying out a garden hose or a rope, you can play with the shape until it's exactly what you want.

Step #2 Dig the outer edge of the pond before removing your perimeter marker. This will ensure that you don't lose the shape.

Step #3 Continue to excavate the hole. Here I'm removing the sod for the flat rock border.

Step #4 It's important to note that I'm leveling just the front part of the pond, because we're doing a flat rock border. By using a large 2X4 and a spirit level, I can get the pond level to within an inch or two, which is close enough at this point.

Step #5 We are going to put a shelf on the back wall of the pond. This shelf is for marginal plants as well as boulders. Here I'm making sure that the shelf is approximately ten inches deep and ten inches wide.

Step #6 Now it's time to prepare the excavated hole for the pond liner. Here I'm using two to four inches of sand on the bottom and old burlap sacks on the sides.

Step#7 Now put your pond liner in. Be sure that there is plenty of overlap all the way around. Because of this pond's unique shape, it will be necessary to make some creases; as I'm doing here.

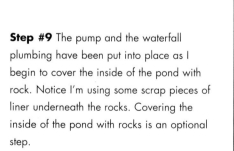

Step #8 Because of the free form shape, there will be some excess liner. Some of this excess can be cut (stay at least twelve inches away from the edge of the pond) and used inside the pond as a buffer between the boulders and the pond liner.

Step #9 The pump and the waterfall plumbing have been put into place as I begin to cover the inside of the pond with rock. Notice I'm using some scrap pieces of liner underneath the rocks. Covering the inside of the pond with rocks is an optional step.

Step #10 Only the back of the pond is completely rocked in this case, because we're doing an overhanging flat rock border in the front. You may choose to rock the entire pond, or maybe just from the shelf up.

Step #11 After all of the rock has been carefully placed inside the pond, you may begin filling. Notice the plumbing in the background is completely hidden by rock as it comes out of the pond.

Step #12 Now that the pond is full of water, we can trim back the excess liner being sure to stay at least six to eight inches back from the edge of the water.

Step #13 If you choose to do a flat rock border, this is the most important step. The water will show you the exact level. When the water is cresting the entire area that you want level, you know it's perfect.

Here are the elements needed to do a flat rock border. A shovel for carrying the mortar, a garden hoe for mixing, a hand trowel for finishing work, pre-mix mortar, and the rock of your choice.

Step #14 Drain the pond down six inches or so to keep the mortar out of the water. To begin, lay a bed of mortar about one inch thick. Note: Always wear gloves when working with any cement type product.

Step #15 When placing the first rock in the bed of mortar be sure that it has two to three inches of overhang.

Step #16 After placing the second rock you can backfill any gaps with the mortar. Pat the mortar with a wet glove until you get a smooth finish. Notice how the front of the rocks are lined up.

Step #17 Let the mortar set up for about an hour and then, using a trowel, make a nice smooth cut along the back. This gives the border a finished look.

Step #18 No pond is complete without landscaping. This includes water plants as well as plantings around the pond. Landscaping around the water feature might best be described as putting the icing on the cake.

Behold! The final result of your work is a beautiful pond that will bring you and your family years of enjoyment. The pond will be the focal point of the entire landscape; it will never go unnoticed.

Bringing greenery and color
right up to the pond is a
very important part
of the overall look.

Installing a Preformed Pond

STEP #1 Before excavating the hole, set the pond on the proposed site, turn the pond upside-down and mark the outer edge using ground marking paint or flour.

STEP #2 Begin excavation. Dig slightly wider and deeper than the pond requires. If the preformed pond has a shelf, dig to that level, then stop.

STEP #3 Place the pond back in the partially excavated hole and mark around the deeper level.

STEP #4 Finish the excavation. Now put one to two inches of clean sand on the bottom of the hole and on the shelves. This will protect the liner shell from rocks or any other hard objects in the soil.

STEP #5 Level the excavated area as much as possible before placing the pond in. It's best to use a spirit level and a straight 2x4 board.

STEP #6 Fill the pond slowly, constantly checking level. As the pond is filling with water, backfill around the pond with a sandy loam or plain sand. It is important to pack the backfill material firmly to avoid any settling.

STEP #7 Now the pond is full and completely level. Hide the edges using a flat stone or plantings that will overhang, concealing the edge of the pond. Add the pump, filter, plants and fish.

The reward; a perfect pond that appears to have been professionally installed.

Large Ponds

On larger jobs it's best to use a small backhoe for the bulk of the digging, although you will still need to get into the hole with a shovel to do all the fine tuning.

Below, an electronic laser level is being used to ensure that the desired level is always known by those doing the excavating.

Waterfall Building

Moving water. This is the pinnacle of the water feature. A waterfall/stream that is built correctly should make anyone stop in their tracks to appreciate its magnificence.

This chapter is the most comprehensive how-to on waterfalls that you'll ever see. By using these methods, you'll not only have a beautiful waterfall, but it will also be built to last.

This unique waterfall was made by hollowing out the center of a lightweight feather rock to form a holding pool.
The rock was bored out using wood carving tools. This is a perfect example of the holding pool doing its job. Because the water is being shot into a holding pool first, the water is allowed to flow out of the rock with an even, natural look.

This waterfall is going to be built with the dirt that was excavated from the pond.

Step #1 This close-up shows the rock retaining wall behind our mound of dirt. By using a retaining wall behind our falls, there's no need to worry about settling or washing away.

Step #2 Now carve steps into the hillside. Dig the entire stream down six to ten inches. Behind the first drop at the top is a small holding pool. This pool, where everything starts, is to ensure that the water doesn't shoot down the falls straight out of the pipe.

Step #3 The liner is put in place to contour the falls. Make sure there's plenty of liner overhanging the edges. Note how the waterfall liner overlaps (shingle effect) down over the pond liner. This is to make sure, that if it ever leaks, the water still ends up in the pond.

Step #4 The cement work is done right on top of the liner. Pre-mix mortar is being used here. If you would like to mix your own... (3 parts sand / 1 part cement).

Step #5 We are using a thin slate rock for the falls. The slate is placed onto a thin bed of mortar, then leveled both lengthwise and widthwise.

Step #6 Because the slate is laid in mortar, the water will be forced over the top. Next, by mortaring small stones on each side of the slate, the water will be forced down the middle of the rock.

Step #7 Follow this procedure with all the steps (falls) and allow to dry for at least forty-eight hours. Now all the mortar work is done.

Step #8 After waiting a couple of days, start the waterfall. This is a very exciting moment. Notice how none of the excess liner has been trimmed yet. Always run the stream before cutting any liner. This way you'll know what your water level is beforehand.

Step #9 Now trim the excess liner off, staying four to six inches away from water level. Place the rest of the rock in the stream to cover up the existing liner.

Step #10 Add the surrounding landscape, and the job is finished. What you now have is a beautiful waterfall that is built to last.

This single sheet of water drops over five feet before it hits the pond. It's really necessary to have a large natural hill to do something this big. Remember to focus on making your waterfall beautiful. Big is not important, but beautiful is.

There is a strong Northwest feel to this pond located in the State of Washington. This look is achieved by using native rocks and plants.

Filtration

MECHANICAL: A mechanical filter is designed for particle filtration. Mechanical filters collect large debris such as fallen leaves, pine needles and dead foliage. Some mechanical filters are also designed to collect much smaller particles like sludge and some types of algae.

BIOLOGICAL: A biological filter is necessary in a fish pond for two reasons. First, it aids in keeping the pond water healthy. Secondly, a bio-filter will help keep the water clear. Most bio-filters double as mechanical filters.

The general rule is this. If you are planning to have fish, you need a quality biological filtration system. If you are not going to have fish, the need for a bio-filter is lessened. A fish pond without a biological filter is more likely to be unbalanced and diseased. When fish are present, so is fish waste, thus the need for a biological filter. Fish waste breaks down into ammonia (NH_3), which is very toxic to fish. Ammonia is also a result of decomposing material at the bottom of the pond (leaves,

LISA KLEIN

A biological filter keeps the water healthy for the fish and clear for you to see and enjoy them.

excess fish food, tree needles, etc.). Special beneficial bacteria (anaerobic bacteria) that form in the filter media turn this ammonia into nitrites (NO_2). Nitrites are toxic to fish as well, but as the filtration process continues, the nitrites are broken down further into nitrates (NO_3). Nitrates are relatively harmless and are used as

Pictured is a TetraPond biofilter (not yet installed).

food by plants, thereby completing the "nitrogen cycle" (below) and balancing the pond's ecology. Some filters also

NITROGEN CYCLE

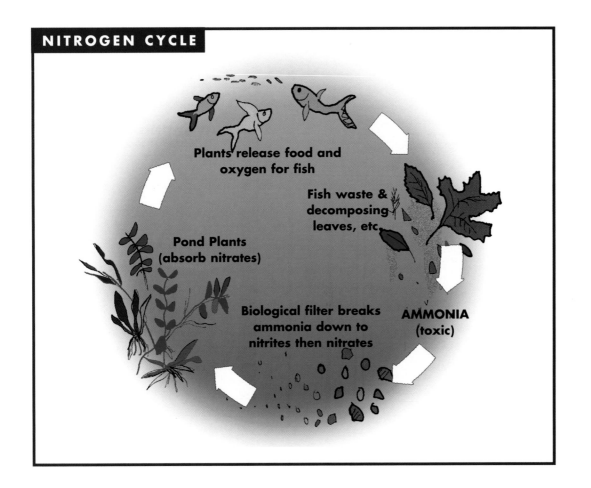

Plants release food and oxygen for fish

Fish waste & decomposing leaves, etc.

Pond Plants (absorb nitrates)

Biological filter breaks ammonia down to nitrites then nitrates

AMMONIA (toxic)

use activated carbon as a media. While the beneficial bacteria break waste down, the activated carbon absorbs it. Filters using this method can be very effective at keeping the water healthy and clear.

As you can see, without a quality biological filter, it is nearly impossible to have a healthy fish pond.

If you are not going to have fish or plants in your pond, chemicals can be used to keep the water clear.

Ultraviolet Lights

The ultraviolet clarifier (UVC) has many jobs, although it is most widely used for clearing pea soup colored ponds. The UVC will eliminate green water and is lethal to all forms of free floating bacteria, harmful and beneficial. If you are using an ultraviolet light in conjunction with a biological filtration system, allow the system to run for a few months before you activate your UVC light. This will enable the beneficial bacteria to pass through the UV chamber unharmed so they can attach themselves to your filter media.

This double waterfall is being viewed from a wooden deck. It's as nice to listen to as it is to look at.

Pond Plants

Floating Plants

Floating plants are simply what their name states. They are not planted in any soil, rather they use their buoyant leaves to float on the surface. The roots hang freely in the water providing small fish with a place to hide. They are also a favorite place for koi and goldfish to lay their eggs. Water lettuce (Pistia Stratiotes) and water hyacinths (Eichhornia spp.) are two favorite examples. Be aware that there are some problems associated with certain species of floaters. Duckweed (Lemna spp.) and Fairy Moss (Azolla spp.) are two specific plants you may want to avoid due to their invasive nature. They can multiply rapidly and completely cover a pond's surface.

Water hyacinths, water lilies, and parrot's feather completely cover this ponds surface.

Water Lilies

(Nymphaea)

The queen of pond plants – her beauty is unmatched. Floating lush green leaves, big and strong, so much so that these seemingly weightless leaves provide a nice resting spot for even the large bullfrog. The vividly colored flowers are most impressive and oftentimes fragrant. The bloom, whether snow white or brilliant red, is a must for any pond. The lily's foliage sweeps across the surface of the pond providing cover for fish. The large round leaves provide protection from the sun as well as predators. As with all pond plants, fertilizing will enhance their beauty.

Marginal Plants

Marginal plants grow in the shallows of the pond, perhaps on a shelf. Most marginal plants do best with a one to two inch water depth over the soil in their

What a sight! A large bullfrog relaxing in the summer sun.

containers. A majority of these attractive marsh plants are hardy and grow rapidly. The Yellow

POND PLANTS

Different types of pond plants and where they belong in the pond.

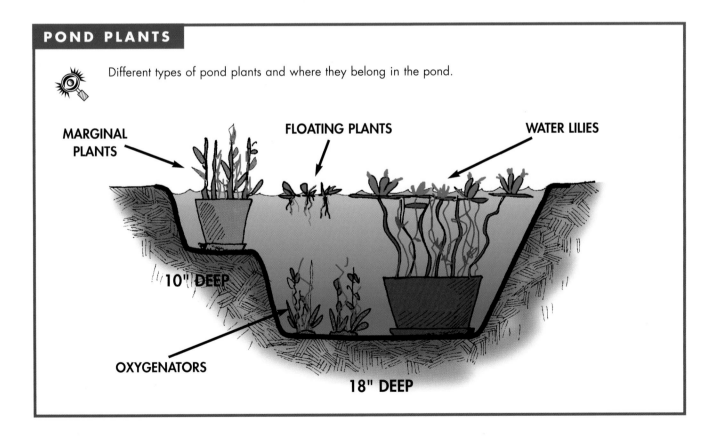

MARGINAL PLANTS

FLOATING PLANTS

WATER LILIES

10" DEEP

OXYGENATORS

18" DEEP

55

Flag Iris (Iris Pseudacorus), Cattails (Typha spp.), and Sweet Flag Iris (Acorus Calamus) are best known for this. Being perennial, they multiply and become more impressive every year. Marginal plants also contribute in creating a natural ecosystem. They remove excess nutrients from the pond water that might otherwise feed algae. Many of these plants grow quite tall. It is best to keep them at the back of the pond so as not to impede the view. Because of the wide variety of marsh plants available with different sizes, shapes, and colors, they make the perfect backdrop to any pond.

This handsome pond is heavily planted and it looks great.

These pond fish hide under the lily pads to get some shade from the hot summer sun.

Oxygenating Plants

Oxygenators (submerged plants) are perhaps the most important of all the pond plants. They're important because of what they do for the ecosystem. These plants absorb dissolved minerals in the water that might otherwise become toxic. In short, oxygenators act very similar to a biological filter. They transpire directly into the water contributing to the total oxygen supply, which is very beneficial to all living organisms in the pond.

The proper rate for stocking these plants is; one bundle for every square foot of surface area.

Fish

Adding fish to the garden pond may be the most enjoyable part of the entire pond experience. There are many different types of fish available for your pond. The two best, and the most popular, are goldfish and koi.

The biggest factor in successfully keeping any fish is water quality. Maintaining a healthy ecological balance is of the utmost importance. This is where a biological filter fits into the picture (Pages 49-51).

Water plants also play a very important role in fish health. It is nearly impossible to overplant your pond as far as your ecological system is concerned. Most healthy natural ponds have

Koi can grow to be very large, oftentimes exceeding thirty inches in length.

between eight to fifteen pounds of aquatic plants per every pound of fish. This is a good lesson to learn from mother nature. Pond plants help absorb nutrients that might otherwise feed algae. Many types of aquatic plants are also beneficial at keeping ammonia levels down, which in turn benefits not only the fish but the entire ecological system.

Oxygen is a necessity for fish. The more surface area a pond has, the more oxygen it will naturally receive. It is very important, and sometimes vital, to have an additional oxygen source, such as a waterfall or fountain, to aerate twenty-four hours a day, because the fish constantly need oxygen.

Goldfish

This most common pond fish is available in many varieties including fantails, sarasa comets (red & white), and shubunkins. Goldfish are easy to keep and they add stunning color to any pond. They are also effective in keeping the bug population down, as mosquito larva is a favorite meal. Most varieties of goldfish will not outgrow their pond. Fancy varieties, such as the lionhead and black moor, don't do well in cooler climates. They are not as hardy.

These fish seem to be suspended in mid-air as they gracefully swim through the crystal clear water.

Koi

The two varieties are Domestic, "locally bred" and Imported, usually coming from Japan. Even though they are the same basic fish on the inside, they are quite different in physical appearance. Imported koi have more brilliant well-defined color patterns. Koi are noted for making great pets. They can be taught to eat right out of their owner's hand. That's quite a thrill! Koi and goldfish coexist well together as long as the koi are not too large. Large koi tend to be heavy feeders and may not leave much food for their small friends. Just as with goldfish, koi will not outgrow their pond.

Look at these koi jumping right into the hand that feeds them!

KEY NOTE

If you are going to keep fish you'll need three things:

1. A quality biological filtration system
2. Pond plants
3. Oxygen / Aeration

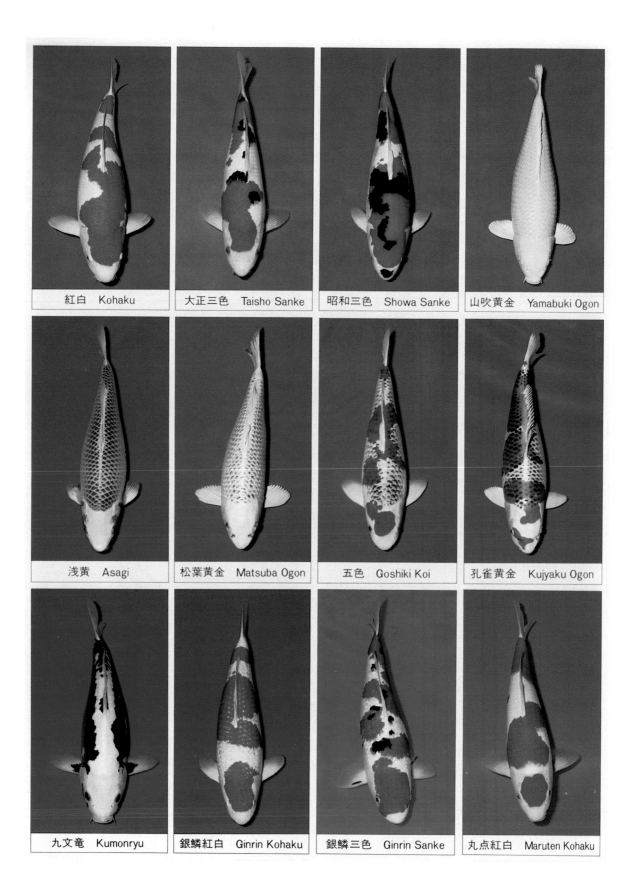

紅白　Kohaku	大正三色　Taisho Sanke	昭和三色　Showa Sanke	山吹黄金　Yamabuki Ogon
浅黄　Asagi	松葉黄金　Matsuba Ogon	五色　Goshiki Koi	孔雀黄金　Kujyaku Ogon
九文竜　Kumonryu	銀鱗紅白　Ginrin Kohaku	銀鱗三色　Ginrin Sanke	丸点紅白　Maruten Kohaku

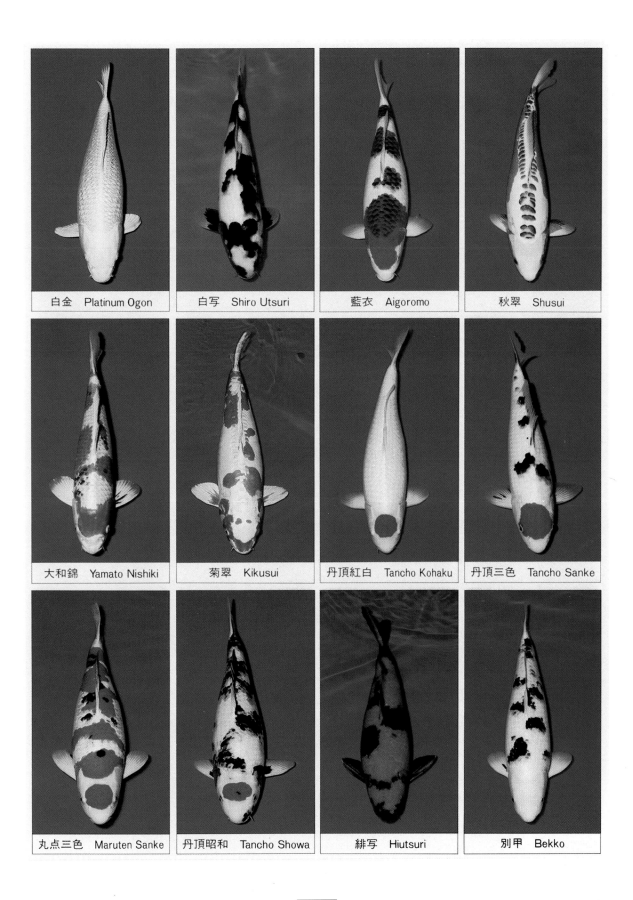

白金 Platinum Ogon	白写 Shiro Utsuri	藍衣 Aigoromo	秋翠 Shusui
大和錦 Yamato Nishiki	菊翠 Kikusui	丹頂紅白 Tancho Kohaku	丹頂三色 Tancho Sanke
丸点三色 Maruten Sanke	丹頂昭和 Tancho Showa	緋写 Hiutsuri	別甲 Bekko

This is the most enjoyable time of the day.

Koi are bred for their distinct color patterns.

Stocking The Pond

There are many mathematical rules and calculations as to how many fish to add in relation to the size of the pond. Most of these rules are difficult to understand or are just plain inaccurate. The key is to stock the pond slowly allowing the pond's ecology to develop. Do not add too many fish too quickly. This will put a strain on the ecological system no matter how good your biological filter is. About the best rule to follow is; one inch of fish for every two square feet of surface area, but even this guideline doesn't take into consideration the girth of the fish.

If you focus more on keeping your pond healthy and clear and less on the total number of fish, you will have a successful healthy pond.

KEY NOTE

Do not overfeed pond fish. This will strain your filtration system and cloud the water. As a general rule, feed once a day what the fish eat in three to five minutes. Remember, in most ponds there are plenty of bugs, plants and algae for your fish to eat. Do not feed the fish if the pond water is below fifty degrees. Fish are ectotherms, which means they cannot control their own body temperature. Their digestive systems do not work well when they are cold, so feeding at this time could be detrimental to the fish.

Algae

lgae is the pond owners
most common enemy.
Pond specialty stores and nurs-
eries will field more questions
about algae every year than any
other pond related problem.
Most of the time algae is not as
much a problem as a nuisance.
It does happen, but is generally
not dangerous. It may clog filters, hinder some aquatic plant
growth, or look unsightly.

The main complaint about
algae is "it looks bad." Algae is
very easy to deal with and control, once you know what kind
of algae you're dealing with.

SINGLE CELL ALGAE (pea
soup colored water): This type
of algae turns the pond water
green. It is normally not harmful to fish.

FILAMENTOUS ALGAE
(blanketweed, string algae): This

The string algae on this rock may be unsightly, but it is harmless.

is the green slime that forms on
the rocks and side walls of your
pond. Filamentous algae is a
sign of healthy water and, it
does benefit your pond by
removing excess ammonia.
Also, where you find this type
of algae, you also find clear
water. Best case scenario -
remove the blanketweed by

hand. An algicide is always your
last choice.

Algae cannot be completely
avoided in a fish pond, but it can
be controlled. Algae needs sunlight to reproduce and thrive.
You can shade most of the pond
by covering approximately two-
thirds of the pond's surface with
plants, such as water lilies, water

hyacinth, and water lettuce. Also, dyeing the pond water with a nontoxic ultraviolet sunscreen will help to shade the pond from the sun's rays that promote algae growth. Heavy planting with aquatic plants will help keep algae at a minimum, because they will compete with the algae for available nutrients. Without aquatic plants all of the available nutrients feed the algae. Submerged plants (oxygenators) like Dwarf Sagittaria and Anacharis will also be a great help. They compete directly with the algae for available nutrients more than any other

Long meandering streams like this one can be magnets for string algae.

type of plant. These oxygenators may need to be replaced every so often due to the fact the fish like to eat them.

KEY NOTE

Algae Control

1. A quality biological filtration system.

2. Shade the pond.

3. Use aquatic plants.

4. Prepackaged enzymes and bacteria.

Seasonal Care

Winter

The magic number is "50". Most pond fish (koi, goldfish, etc.) become dormant in the wintertime when the water temperature cools to below 50 degrees. Fish will go into a hibernation state during this time. Do not feed them once the water cools to below 50 degrees, because their cold bodies have a difficult time digesting the food. In all but the coldest regions, it is important to leave the pump running all through the winter. This way you're still getting the most enjoyment out of your water feature and are also continuing to aerate the water. Biological filters are barely effective in the winter due to the fact that the beneficial bacteria that make them so effective all spring and summer die in the cold water or, at best, become dormant. Most biological filters also do quite a bit of mechanical filtration as well. By running the pump through your filter year-round, you're able to keep the pond relatively clear of floating debris. If you do decide to turn your pump off and let the pond freeze over, try to keep a section of the pond clear of ice by using a pond heater or by boiling water and then holding the pot on the ice. By keeping a hole open you are allowing toxins, which are harmful to the fish, an opportunity to escape and oxygen to enter the pond.

It doesn't matter whether it's the middle of summer (above) or the dead of winter (below).
This pond and fountain are always elegant.

Spring

The pond comes back to life around 50 degrees. The fish will become active and want to eat. It is best to start them off with a food that is easy to digest like a wheatgerm or staple food. Since the fish are just coming out of dormancy, they are very weak and susceptible to disease. It's best to treat the pond water for disease as a preventive measure in early spring.

All the marginal plants begin to sprout new growth and the long arms of the water lily are reaching for the surface now. Perennials come back every spring and what a delight it is to watch them grow!

It's fun to check the pond daily while waiting for the first blooms of the year to appear. Marsh Marigolds (Caltha spp.) followed by the Water Iris are the first you'll see.

In most parts of North

America floating plants are annuals. Once all threat of frost is gone, you can purchase water hyacinths and water lettuce.

In early springtime the fish, plants, and biological filter begin to wake up the pond. Spring is a good time to kick start your biological filter by adding starter cultures (beneficial bacteria). Your filter will form these on its own over time, but by adding commercially available bacteria and enzymes, you instantly age your pond, giving your filter the ability to immediately remove toxins from the water.

This is also a great time to do a partial water change to remove any debris that entered the pond during the winter.

Every spring this Japanese Maple creeps down into the water. Leafy trees like this one provide shade and elegance.

Summer

Definitely the most wonderful time of the year for enjoying your pond. The fish are active and growing. Pond plants are full of blooms and their foliage is thick. On a summer night you leave your windows open to enjoy the tranquil sound of moving water. A pond's brilliance and elegance are magnified this time of year. Your garden pond is at its peak.

Be aware of evaporation. Be sure to treat the water with a dechlorinator / heavy metal neutralizer every time you top the pond off with your garden hose.

Fall

The pond will require some preparation for its winter rest. As plant foliage begins to turn brown, it can be cut back (example: trimming your roses down before winter). In colder climates drop the plant baskets down to the bottom of the pond to prevent the roots from freezing. As the plants become dormant, so will your fish.

The flowers really enhance this small brook.

This quiet pond is a calming place to spend some time at the end of the day.

Accessories

Once your pond has been completely installed, nothing is more fun than adding accessories. Of course, adding fish and plants is part of it, but there is so much more available.

How you choose to landscape and decorate around your pond will depend on whether you want a natural setting or something more formal.

Here are a few clever ways to enhance your water feature.

A half whiskey barrel makes the ultimate patio pond.

a pond / waterfall is even more beautiful in the dark of night. Lighting the pond is not a scientific endeavor. There is no right or wrong way of doing it. You be the judge of what you want. Some will choose to highlight their waterfall or maybe light up some nearby trees to reflect on the pond's surface. Others will opt for underwater lighting. All of these options are winners and are equally impressive.

Lighting

Without lighting in the pond's landscape, you miss its beauty and tranquility at night. All that impresses and is enjoyed throughout the day disappears. A water feature is the focal point of any landscape and should be featured at night, as well as during the day. Many agree that with proper lighting

Fountains

Fountains come in such a wide range of options that the choices are limitless. Fountains can be a focal point of any for-

mal water feature but, when used in conjunction with a waterfall, can seriously detract from a natural setting, because of the way many of them look and sound. Remember that fountains are usually associated with formal water features.

This fountain provides an interesting look.

Bridges

If you decide to place a bridge over the pond, make it sturdy, because they seem to beg people to walk across them. Everyone loves to stand on a bridge and look down on the water below, or feed the fish from this most spectacular vantage point. A key point to remember is; a bridge takes some of the surface area out of view. On a small pond this can really cover up a large area. That

This strong bridge is made of natural stone.

being said, bridging water is generally a winning idea that looks great.

Pond lighting is, in a word; impressive.

Your Pond Information

Dimensions: _____

Total Gallons: _____

Pump Size: _____

Filter Type: _____

Plumbing Type: _____

Pond Fish (breed & stocking): _____

_____

_____

_____

_____

_____

Pond Plants: _____

_____

_____

_____

_____

Your Pond Information
Seasonal Care

Spring: _____

_____

_____

_____

Summer: _____

_____

_____

_____

Winter: _____

_____

_____

_____

Fall: _____

_____

_____

_____

Water Feature Design

Water Feature Design

Water Feature Design

Water Feature Design

Water Feature Design

Water Feature Design

Index